Adrenaline Adventure

Pulling the Rip Cord:
Skydiving

Pro-tec

Jeff C. Young
ABDO Publishing Company

visit us at
www.abdopublishing.com

Published by ABDO Publishing Company, 8000 West 78th Street, Edina, Minnesota 55439.
Copyright © 2011 by Abdo Consulting Group, Inc. International copyrights reserved in all
countries. No part of this book may be reproduced in any form without written permission from the
publisher. The Checkerboard Library™ is a trademark and logo of ABDO Publishing Company.

Printed in the United States of America, North Mankato, Minnesota.
092010
012011

 PRINTED ON RECYCLED PAPER

Cover Photo: Thinkstock
Interior Photos: Alamy pp. 1, 6–7, 8–9, 9, 13, 14, 19, 20–21, 24, 27; AP Images p. 23;
     Bodyflight Ltd. pp. 5, 25, 29; Getty Images p. 22; iStockphoto pp. 28, 31; Jupiterimages p. 12;
     Photolibrary pp. 10, 10–11, 17

Series Coordinator: Heidi M.D. Elston
Editors: Heidi M.D. Elston, Megan M. Gunderson, BreAnn Rumsch
Art Direction & Cover Design: Neil Klinepier

Library of Congress Cataloging-in-Publication Data

Young, Jeff C., 1948-
 Pulling the rip cord : skydiving / Jeff C. Young.
    p. cm. -- (Adrenaline adventure)
 ISBN 978-1-61613-550-8
 1. Skydiving--Juvenile literature. I. Title.
 GV770.Y68 2011
 797.5--dc22

                    2010028243

Contents

First to Fly

Long before airplanes were invented, people used parachutes. In fact, parachute use dates as far back as the 1100s. People in China used them to jump from towers and buildings.

In 1797, Frenchman André-Jacques Garnerin performed the first parachute jump from an aircraft. He leaped from a hot air balloon over Paris, France.

In 1903, Orville and Wilbur Wright made the first successful airplane flight. As airplanes became more common, so did parachutes.

Parachutes first aided military forces during **World War I**. After the war, **barnstormers** made parachute use even more popular. They traveled around the United States demonstrating parachute jumps.

Soon, parachute competitions began. The first accuracy landing competition was in 1930 at the Sports Festival in the **USSR**. Two years later, the first parachute competition in the United States was held.

After **World War II**, there was a **surplus** of parachutes and former soldiers with jumping experience. This led to the growth of parachuting as a hobby.

In the mid-1950s, parachute jumpers began calling the sport *skydiving*. Since that time, the sport has gained a worldwide following. For those seeking adventure, pulling the rip cord is a thrilling experience!

You're never too young to start learning about skydiving!

Free Fall!

There are several different types of skydiving. Casual weekend jumpers and professionals can take their pick! Beginners can choose from tandem, static-line, and accelerated free fall (AFF) jumps.

A tandem jump offers the first-time skydiver the chance to experience free fall. This is the time between exiting an aircraft and the parachute opening. Free fall can last a few seconds to more than one minute!

In a tandem jump, the first-time jumper is not alone. He or she is attached to the front of an experienced instructor. The instructor does the work. The student gets to enjoy the ride!

Once the **canopy** is open, the instructor may let the student steer. These jumps are made from at least 7,500 feet (2,280 m). They last for about four minutes.

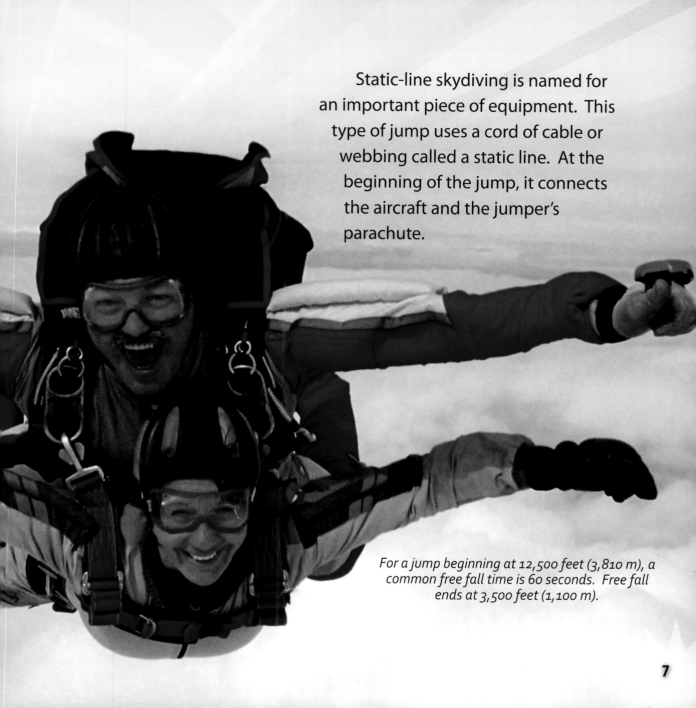

Static-line skydiving is named for an important piece of equipment. This type of jump uses a cord of cable or webbing called a static line. At the beginning of the jump, it connects the aircraft and the jumper's parachute.

For a jump beginning at 12,500 feet (3,810 m), a common free fall time is 60 seconds. Free fall ends at 3,500 feet (1,100 m).

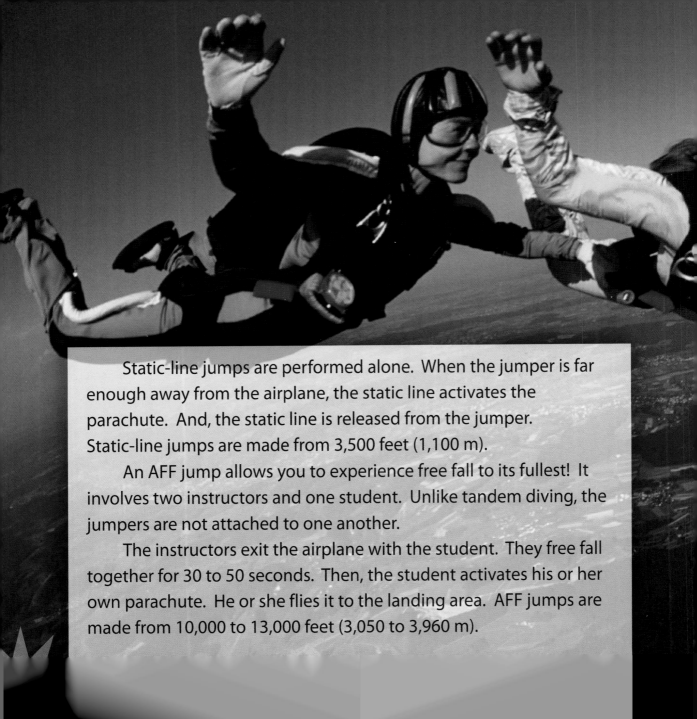

Static-line jumps are performed alone. When the jumper is far enough away from the airplane, the static line activates the parachute. And, the static line is released from the jumper. Static-line jumps are made from 3,500 feet (1,100 m).

An AFF jump allows you to experience free fall to its fullest! It involves two instructors and one student. Unlike tandem diving, the jumpers are not attached to one another.

The instructors exit the airplane with the student. They free fall together for 30 to 50 seconds. Then, the student activates his or her own parachute. He or she flies it to the landing area. AFF jumps are made from 10,000 to 13,000 feet (3,050 to 3,960 m).

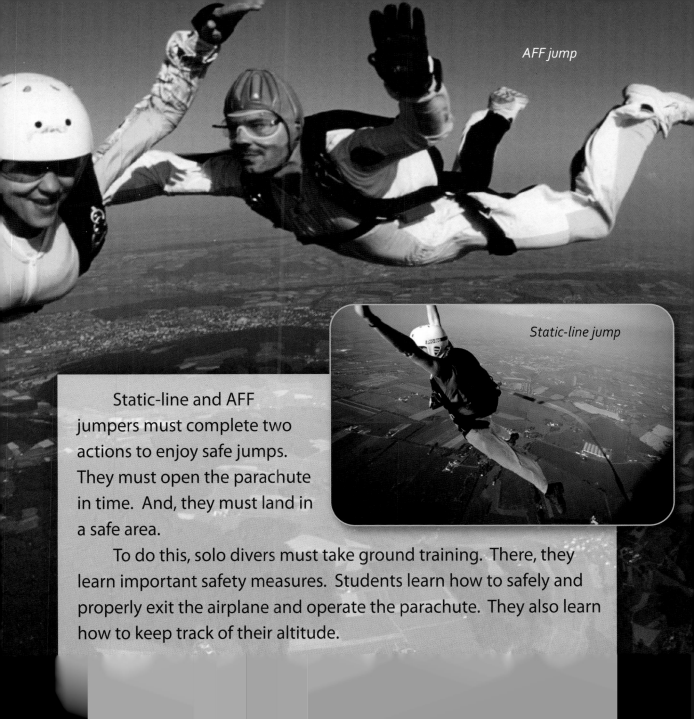

AFF jump

Static-line jump

Static-line and AFF jumpers must complete two actions to enjoy safe jumps. They must open the parachute in time. And, they must land in a safe area.

To do this, solo divers must take ground training. There, they learn important safety measures. Students learn how to safely and properly exit the airplane and operate the parachute. They also learn how to keep track of their altitude.

Cords & Chutes

To skydive, a skydiver needs more than just a parachute and an airplane. Special equipment helps make jumps safe and successful.

The parachute and the equipment that makes it work is called a rig. Rigs differ slightly depending on the type of skydiving. But, they all have the same basic parts.

All skydivers wear two parachutes. These are the main and the reserve parachutes. The main parachute is the one that opens up during the jump.

The reserve is an emergency backup. It opens

A skydiver's gear costs $2,000 to $6,000.

if the main parachute fails to open. The reserve is like a spare tire on a car. Skydivers hope to never have to use it. But it's good to have one, just in case.

A special harness container holds the main and reserve parachutes. This attaches to the jumper's backpack. A harness then straps the backpack to the jumper. The harness buckles around his or her thighs, chest, and shoulders.

PACKING FOR PROTECTION

The Federal Aviation Administration (FAA) requires the reserve parachute to be inspected and repacked every 180 days. Only federally certified parachute riggers can pack reserve parachutes. This is just one of the many rules that keep skydivers safe.

The pilot chute is a small parachute. It gets the main parachute to open. Some skydivers release the pilot chute by hand. Other pilot chutes pop open when the skydiver pulls the rip cord. Pulling this small handle activates the parachute.

One of the most important things to know is when to pull the rip cord. That's why skydivers use an altimeter. This tool measures altitude. A skydiver reads it to know when to open the parachute.

An altimeter shows a skydiver his or her altitude.

Altimeters may be worn on the wrist like a watch. They can also be worn on the chest. Some are mounted on a helmet. These make a beeping sound. That reminds the jumper when to open the parachute.

Many skydivers also use an automatic activation device (AAD). This small computer keeps track of a skydiver's altitude and descent rate. The AAD senses if the rate of descent is near free fall speed after falling below normal opening altitude. If this happens, the AAD releases one of the parachutes.

The pilot chute is attached to the main parachute by fabric webbing called a bridle. When the pilot chute inflates in the air, the main parachute container is triggered open.

A special wing suit allows a skydiver to fall at a slower rate.

A very important piece of skydiving equipment is the airplane! The best airplanes for the sport have high wings and wide doorways. And, they are able to cruise at slow speeds. Small, one-propeller planes are popular. Some big skydiving competitions use two-engine planes. These can carry more jumpers.

Nearly any type of clothing is suitable for skydiving. However, most people wear a one-piece jumpsuit. The design of the jumpsuit varies for different types of skydiving. Skydivers who make formations in the air with other divers wear jumpsuits with special grips. The grips make it easier for them to hold on to one another.

Most skydivers wear lightweight shoes such as sneakers. Jumpers should never wear shoes with open hooks for laces. The hooks could catch on a parachute as it is opening.

Skydivers need protective gear for their heads. Helmets made of hard plastic or leather protect them from unexpected dangers. Goggles protect their eyes from rushing winds and objects in the air.

Training

Have you decided to commit to skydiving? Over time, you'll probably want to improve your performance. You will learn to jump at different altitudes and in different conditions. The more you jump and practice, the better you will become.

As skydivers gain experience, they can become licensed by the United States Parachute Association (USPA). The USPA offers training and instructor qualification programs.

The USPA has four different classes of licenses. Higher-level licenses allow skydivers to become instructors and coaches. They also allow divers to compete in skydiving events.

After 25 jumps, a skydiver can earn an A license. This allows skydivers to jump without **supervision**. They can also pack their own main parachutes. And, they can perform water jumps.

To earn a B license, a person must complete 50 jumps. This allows a diver to perform night jumps. After 200 jumps, the skydiver earns a C license. A diver obtains a D license after completing 500 jumps.

As skydivers become more skilled, they can begin doing group jumps.

Get Competitive

Competition has become popular in skydiving. There are local and international contests. Throughout the United States, the USPA **sanctions** competitions. Licensed skydivers can choose from a variety of individual and team events.

Formation skydiving and **canopy** formation are popular team events. Formation skydiving involves teams of 4, 8, or 16. In free fall, the jumpers build patterns by holding on to one another. They build as many formations as they can within a time limit. A team of 4 is allowed 35 seconds. Teams of 8 and 16 get 50 seconds.

Teams of 2, 4, or 8 compete in canopy formation. They build formations after their parachutes are open. For both events, judges award points for style, difficulty, and number of formations completed.

Skydivers in canopy formation

19

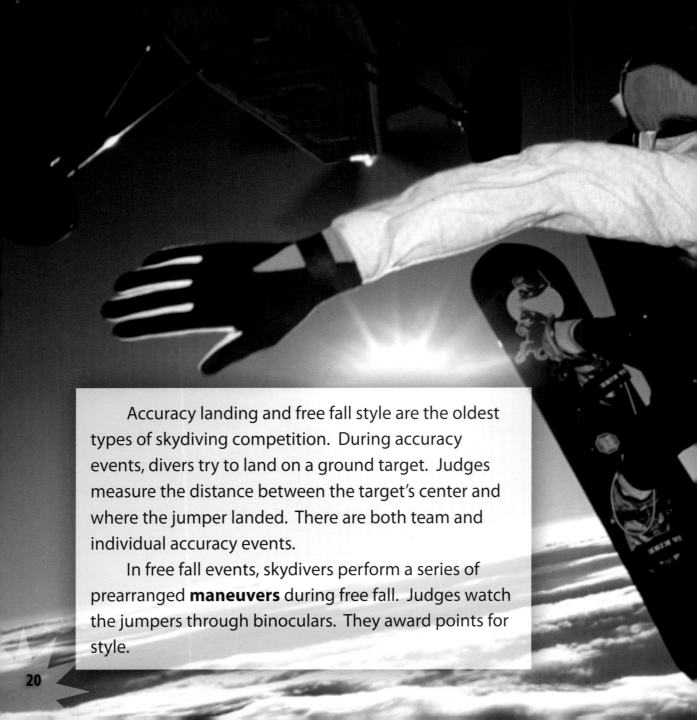

Accuracy landing and free fall style are the oldest types of skydiving competition. During accuracy events, divers try to land on a ground target. Judges measure the distance between the target's center and where the jumper landed. There are both team and individual accuracy events.

In free fall events, skydivers perform a series of prearranged **maneuvers** during free fall. Judges watch the jumpers through binoculars. They award points for style.

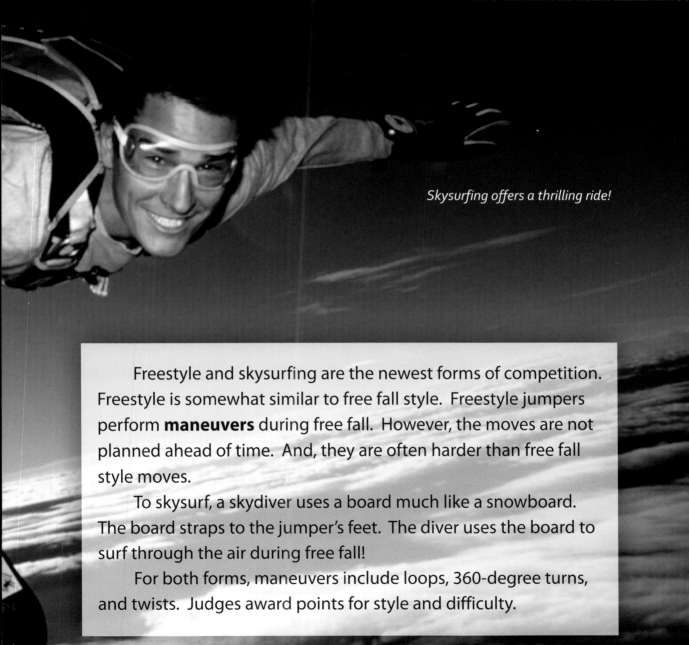

Skysurfing offers a thrilling ride!

     Freestyle and skysurfing are the newest forms of competition. Freestyle is somewhat similar to free fall style. Freestyle jumpers perform **maneuvers** during free fall. However, the moves are not planned ahead of time. And, they are often harder than free fall style moves.

     To skysurf, a skydiver uses a board much like a snowboard. The board straps to the jumper's feet. The diver uses the board to surf through the air during free fall!

     For both forms, maneuvers include loops, 360-degree turns, and twists. Judges award points for style and difficulty.

Famous Flyers

Cheryl Stearns

Skydiving is not as popular as baseball or soccer. But, many skydiving athletes have made fantastic achievements.

Don Kellner and Cheryl Stearns are the world's most experienced skydivers. Kellner has made more than 38,000 jumps. He holds the Guinness World Record for most career total jumps.

Stearns has made the most jumps of any woman. She has jumped more than 17,000 times.

In 2008, Holly Budge became the first woman to skydive in front of Mount Everest. The mountain is the world's tallest. Budge jumped

George H.W. Bush (bottom)

from an altitude of 29,500 feet (9,000 m). She then landed at the world's highest drop zone at 12,350 feet (3,700 m).

Former U.S. president George H.W. Bush turned 85 in June 2009. To celebrate, he made a tandem jump. He jumped with a member of the U.S. Army Golden Knights parachute squad. This was Bush's seventh parachute jump. His first occurred during **World War II**.

Safety First

All forms of skydiving have the same kinds of risks. Strong winds, equipment failure, human error, and crashes can occur. All can lead to injury or even death. The USPA has worked to make skydiving as safe as possible for every jumper.

Every skydiver must follow a few rules every time they jump. Skydivers should never attempt a jump under the influence of alcohol or drugs. They should avoid jumping in dangerous conditions. These include strong winds and storms. Divers should avoid jumping when sick, too. Jumping with a head cold could lead to eardrum damage.

For safety, first-time jumpers practice the basic free fall position. This face-to-earth position offers stability and a great view!

Skydivers must always be aware of who and what is around them. Before jumping, skydivers should learn the dangers in the area. These include trees, power lines, highways, and rivers. Learning about the area before a jump will make for a safer landing. Jumpers must also check their gear before each jump.

Don't think that following all these rules will make skydiving less fun. It won't! But it will help keep everyone safe. In skydiving, you risk serious injury or even death by not following the rules.

LINGO

BE CURRENT – to have jumped recently enough to retain proficiency in the sport.

BOOGIE – a gathering of skydivers for the purposes of jumping and socializing.

DIRT DIVE – to practice a skydive on the ground.

DROP ZONE – a skydiving center.

IN DATE – a reserve parachute that has been packed within the previous 180 days.

JUMP MASTER – a jumper who is trained and certified to supervise students and first-time jumpers.

SKYGOD – a skydiver whose ego has grown faster than his or her skydiving ability.

WHUFFO – someone who is not a skydiver.

Drop In!

After reading about skydiving, you might feel ready to make that first jump. It's not too difficult to get started!

First, find a drop zone close to where you live. The USPA can tell you the location of the nearest one. Be sure to ask how old you need to be to make a jump. Some states won't allow anyone under 18 to skydive. Others will allow a 16-year-old to jump with a parent's permission.

There are many stunning drop zones throughout the United States. You can enjoy a view of fields, mountains, or the ocean. The possibilities are endless!

Amazing skydiving views can be found in every state. Free fall over Hawaii's beautiful ocean waters. Experience the Rocky Mountains while gliding under a **canopy**. Check out Florida's Kennedy Space Center as your airplane flies to jump altitude!

Do you have some time before you meet the age limit? You can still practice skydiving! Indoor skydiving centers offer practice day or night in any weather. Flyaway Indoor Skydiving in Tennessee and Skyventure Orlando in Florida are two popular indoor centers.

Indoor skydivers fly on a column of air. They can learn to move through air while practicing control. Diving at an indoor center is helpful. It makes the shift to skydiving at a drop zone much easier.

Getting involved in skydiving gives you the chance to meet other adventurous people. It also helps build your **confidence** in yourself.

There aren't any special warm up exercises for skydiving. You don't have to be a world-class athlete to jump. Some people believe yoga helps improve their skydiving. This form of exercise can help with balance and strengthen muscles. And, it can be done at a drop zone!

Before jumping, it is very important to be mentally prepared. You should be sure that skydiving is something you want to do. Always be ready to follow your instructor's directions. With commitment, the right gear, and lots of practice, you'll soon be ready to pull the rip cord!

TEAM FUTURE

Team Future is the world's youngest skydiving team. Its members are looking forward to making their first jump out of an airplane.

For now, they practice in wind tunnels. A wind tunnel allows them to experience free fall without actually jumping from an airplane. Jumpers don't have to worry about parachutes or landings! They can focus on having fun while perfecting their skills.

The members of Team Future believe kids can skydive just as well as adults. With their work, Team Future hopes to draw attention to young skydivers. And, they work to encourage more kids to take up the sport.

Glossary

barnstormer - someone who tours country towns and rural areas giving exhibitions of stunt flying.

canopy - the fabric part of a parachute that opens up and fills with air.

confidence - faith in oneself and one's powers.

maneuver (muh-NOO-vuhr) - a clever or skillful move or action.

sanction - to approve or authorize.

supervision - care or management.

surplus - an amount above what is needed.

USSR - Union of Soviet Socialist Republics. The USSR was a country in Europe and Asia from 1922 to 1991.

World War I - from 1914 to 1918, fought in Europe. Great Britain, France, Russia, the United States, and their allies were on one side. Germany, Austria-Hungary, and their allies were on the other side.

World War II - from 1939 to 1945, fought in Europe, Asia, and Africa. Great Britain, France, the United States, the Soviet Union, and their allies were on one side. Germany, Italy, Japan, and their allies were on the other side.

Web Sites

To learn more about skydiving, visit ABDO Publishing Company online. Web sites about skydiving are featured on our Book Links page. These links are routinely monitored and updated to provide the most current information available.
www.abdopublishing.com

Index